# Setting Yourself Apart unto God

Book Four of the Duncan-Williams Youth Series

## Archbishop Nicholas Duncan-Williams

A GOSHEN PUBLISHERS PAPERBACK    VIRGINIA

Setting Yourself Apart unto God
Book Four

ISBN: 978-1-7342639-0-9

Published in 2019
by:

GOSHEN PUBLISHERS LLC
P.O. Box 1562
Stephens City, Virginia, USA
www.GoshenPublishers.com

Our books may be purchased in bulk for promotional, educational, or business use. Please email Agents@GoshenPublishers.com.

First Edition 2019

Cover designed by Goshen Publishers LLC

The Duncan-Williams Youth Series seeks, among several others, to bless you in the following ways:

1. Help you totally yield your life and your future to God, trusting and depending wholly on Him;

2. Equip and challenge you to build and maintain a vibrant intimate relationship with God so you can navigate the journey of life more decisively;

3. Help you become a man or woman of prayer, drawing power from your fellowship with God to deal with situations in your life;

4. Get you to pay closer attention to the value of the family of God on earth, so

you can stay with the brethren and not become an easy target of the enemy;

5. Help you identify sin in its forms and resolve to confront sin with the principles and power of God;

6. Dare you to be different in your generation that is heavily influenced by immorality and godlessness, and thereby walk in integrity, honoring God in your life always;

7. Assist you to discover and develop your God-given talents and spiritual gifts by which you can offer acceptable service in the house of God;

8. Help you develop Christian character as the foundation for a future life of

leadership and purpose;

9. Challenge you to share your faith in Christ as per the gospel, and God's power unto salvation without fear, and become a good evangelist for God;

10. Help you know how to draw strength from the holy spirit, stand in the position of authority, and walk in victory in all the issues confronting you as a growing person; and

11. Help you understand and develop healthful habits in relating with the opposite sex, and thereby prepare for a meaningful marriage and family life.

Setting Yourself Apart unto God

Book Four

**Other Publications in this series:**

- ✓ *Book 1: Beginning with God*
- ✓ *Book 2: Becoming a Strong Christian*
- ✓ *Book 3: Developing Intimacy with God*
- ✓ *Book 5: Discovering and Walking in Purpose*

**All by Archbishop Nicholas Duncan-Williams**

# This book belongs to

_____

[Name]

# CONTENTS

INTRODUCTION ..................................................................1

1. THE PRINCIPLE OF BEING SET APART ............................7
   MEN WHOSE CALLING WERE NOT OBVIOUS .....................9
   MEN WHOSE CALLING WAS OBVIOUS ...........................13

2. THE LIFE OF A NAZARITE: ONE SET APART .............31
   NAZARITES UNDER THE NEW TESTAMENT ....................35

3. OVERCOMING YOUTHFUL TEMPTATIONS .................47
   KEEPING YOURSELF PURE ............................................50

4. DON'T GET ENTANGLED ........................................57
   LOVE NOT THE WORLD ...............................................63

5. THE BLESSINGS OF A LIFE OF PURITY ........................69
   A GOOD CONSCIENCE! .................................................74
   FACING LIFE MORE CONFIDENTLY ...............................75
   YOU BECOME ALMOST INCORRUPTIBLE ........................76
   NO MORE DOUBLE MINDEDNESS .................................77
   ASSURANCE OF HEAVEN ..............................................78

6. YOUR PERSONAL NAZARITE VOW ..........................79
   MAKING IT VERY PERSONAL .........................................83

*Duncan-Williams Youth Series: Book One*

# INTRODUCTION

When anything is set apart, it means that thing is specially marked out of the lot for a well-identified purpose. If your mum goes out, for example, finds a jug amongst several on display and selects one and pays for it, that is the first level of setting apart.

She just separated that one from all the others. When she brings it home and declares that only dad will be using this jug to drink, that becomes another level of setting apart. Everyone in the house now sees that jug as dad's, and everyone treats it with respect because it has been designated as his own. You know that dad can travel for six months, for example, and during his absence, no one will dare use the jug.

That is what it means when something is set apart. It is used exclusively for the purpose identified.

It not only happens in our homes that physical items that are set apart for special use. Sometimes it happens outside our homes and we find things set apart for the purpose of blessing humanity.

Setting things apart for special use is actually God's idea. When He created the first humans, named Adam and Eve, God set them apart for something special. They were to dress God's earth and keep it and to dominate it as well.

Since that time, God has always been looking for people to set them apart to do things He wants done on earth for the good of humanity.

God is still looking today for people who are willing to be used by Him to do His work on earth. It is one of the processes God will not pass by. It is an eternal principle.

In this book, I intend to help you understand the principle of being set apart, help you see your life as a believer set apart unto God and what that means for you as a growing person seeking to succeed.

It is my fervent hope that by the time you are through reading, you will have been brought to the point to say, "Here I Am, Lord. I am available, and at Your service, Lord."

# Today, I am willing to be used by God to do His work on earth

_____

[Date]

# 1.

# THE PRINCIPLE OF BEING SET APART

God has followed the principle of setting people apart unto Himself throughout human history. In every generation and depending upon the task to be performed in accordance with His eternal plan, He selects certain individuals and sets them apart.

Some of them are obvious because God specifically announces that He is setting them apart. Some are not obvious but from the way He handles them, it becomes clear that He has chosen to set them apart for His work.

## MEN WHOSE CALLING WERE NOT OBVIOUS

Let us consider Noah, Abraham, Jacob, Joseph, and Moses:

### *Noah*

Concerning Noah, we read that he found favor with the Lord in a generation that had become extremely sinful and rebellious. God commissioned him to build the ark of salvation that had a single door. You know that it was this ark that preserved human life when God's anger was first poured upon humanity by a flood.

## *Jacob*

The Bible says of Jacob that he was preferred to Esau. We know the story of how he disguised himself to receive the blessing that his father thought was to be given to Esau as by their tradition.

In that tradition, the elder is blessed before the latter, but God changed the equation. Don't let the process by which Jacob was blessed instead of Esau cast any doubts in your mind. Call that the sovereignty of God.

God's sovereignty continues to baffle us today. That makes Him God and the rest of us humans. Jacob was God's choice set apart for the purpose of bearing the twelve tribes of Israel.

## *Joseph*

Joseph's experience was another that fits into the category of the non-obvious at the beginning. God did not openly announce He had called Joseph, per se, but God indirectly showed His preference by showing him dreams in which he was ahead of everyone. He did not understand it.

His father also probably did not get it; yet, he turned out to be God's servant set apart for a great purpose. His path initially looked like a path of rejection, until God's plan finally unfolded. Read what he told his brothers:

> 18   *His brothers also came and fell down before him and said, "Behold, we are your servants."*
>
> 19   *But Joseph said to them, "Do not fear, for am I in the place of God?*

<sup>20</sup> *As for you, you meant evil against me, but God meant it for good, to bring it about that many people should be kept alive, as they are today.*

Genesis 50:18-20

## Moses

Moses' mother could never have given an explanation for hiding him when he was born. She probably could not understand to explain to anyone why she put him out in the Nile river. We, who are privileged to read the whole story of Moses, know that God set him apart. Moses also discovered that years later. The climax of it came when God actually called him out of the bush that would not burn.

Moses transitioned from one whose being set apart was not obvious, into the category of the obvious. In his case, being set apart was not communicated to anyone else, just him.

## MEN WHOSE CALLING WAS OBVIOUS

### *Abraham*

For those that God declared as set apart, we can say that Abraham was probably the first. The story is captured in Genesis 12:1-3:

> 1   *The LORD said to Abram, "Leave your country and your people. Leave your father's family and go to the country that I will show you.*
>
> 2   *I will build a great nation from you. I will bless you and make your name famous. People will use your name to bless other people.*
>
> 3   *I will bless those who bless you, and I will curse those who curse you. I will use you to bless all the people on earth."*

God specifically outlined the purpose for calling Abraham. Note that God took him from his country and family of idol worshippers. By the call, God did not expect Abraham to live and worship idols, but to worship Him only. He was to live a life separate from what he saw among his folks and, thus, become an example to the several nations that were going to come out of him. From that time onward, Abraham had no life of his own. His life was what God decided it should be.

If you follow the life of Abraham through his death, you will see his response to God's call. You will see human mistakes once in a while, but you can trace commitment to God's purpose throughout his life. That is why today we talk of the blessing of Abraham coming unto the believers.

## Samuel

Let's start with the story of Samuel.

> [1] *There was a certain man of Ramathaim-zophim of the hill country of Ephraim whose name was*

Elkanah the son of Jeroham, son of Elihu, son of Tohu, son of Zuph, an Ephrathite.

2  He had two wives. The name of the one was Hannah, and the name of the other, Peninnah. And Peninnah had children, but Hannah had no children.

3  Now this man used to go up year by year from his city to worship and to sacrifice to the LORD of hosts at Shiloh, where the two sons of Eli, Hophni and Phinehas, were priests of the LORD.

4  On the day when Elkanah sacrificed, he would give portions to Peninnah his wife and to all her sons and daughters.

5  But to Hannah he gave a double portion, because he loved her,

*though the LORD had closed her womb.*[a]

6 *And her rival used to provoke her grievously to irritate her, because the LORD had closed her womb.*

7 *So it went on year by year. As often as she went up to the house of the LORD, she used to provoke her.*

1 Samuel 1:1-7

There was a man who lived in Israel, called Elkanah, and he had a wife, Hannah. Elkanah had another wife, called Peninah. Elkanah loved Hannah more than Peninah, but Hannah had no children. If you live in my part of the world, you know that this is no fun at all.

The women know what they go through if their rival [husband's other wife] living in the same house has children and she does not have one.

As the story goes, Hannah went through this for several years until one day she decided it was enough. She went to God in prayer like she had always done; and this time, she made an oath before God.

> ⁹ *After they had eaten and drunk in Shiloh, Hannah rose. Now Eli the priest was sitting on the seat beside the doorpost of the temple of the LORD.*
>
> ¹⁰ *She was deeply distressed and prayed to the LORD and wept bitterly.*
>
> ¹¹ *And she vowed a vow and said, "O LORD of hosts, if you indeed look on the affliction of your servant and remember me and not forget your servant, but will give to your servant a son, then I will give him to the LORD all the days of his life, and no razor shall touch his head."*

1 Samuel 1:9-11

Think through Hannah's prayer again. She asked God for a son. She was specific, and we should be specific when we come asking something from God. She was focused on what she knew would gladden God's heart and she plugged her request right in there. Her bargain with God was that if God gave her a boy child, she would dedicate that child to God. It means that child would not own his life but be owned by God.

This is not slavery as when someone sells their children to others for money and their children become the property of the slave master. This, instead, is giving one's property back to the God who gave it in the first place.

Now this is what is called being set apart. It means before Samuel was born, he was already identified as God's own. His life had been bargained already. Believe me it was a good bargain by a woman who knew what she was doing.

Let's get something clear before we move on. It was clear that Hannah's rival, Peninah, had more sons than Hannah; but from the point Samuel was born, no mention was ever made of Peninah and her children for the rest of the lives in Israel. That was God working His sovereign will.

We know the story of Samuel, that he was one of the first prophets of Israel after they had settled in the Promised Land. His life was bargained, and he was set apart for the work of the Lord.

The thing to also note about Samuel was that God began to speak with him when he was only a child. God was going to do something to Israel because they had abandoned His ways and were walking in disobedience. God called little Samuel, who thought it was the high priest Eli who was calling. God bypassed the old high priest to speak serious business with a little child. That is what happens if your life is set apart unto the service of

God. He decides when and what He would do with you out of His sovereign will and plan.

## Samson

The next example of someone being set apart, where God announced His intention was Samson. Let's look at that story, also in the book of Judges:

> ¹ And the people of Israel again did what was evil in the sight of the LORD, so the LORD gave them into the hand of the Philistines for forty years.
>
> ² There was a certain man of Zorah, of the tribe of the Danites, whose name was Manoah. And his wife was barren and had no children.
>
> ³ And the angel of the LORD appeared to the woman and said to her, "Behold, you are barren and have

not borne children, but you shall conceive and bear a son.

4   Therefore be careful and drink no wine or strong drink, and eat nothing unclean,

5   for behold, you shall conceive and bear a son. No razor shall come upon his head, for the child shall be a Nazirite to God from the womb, and he shall begin to save Israel from the hand of the Philistines."

Judges 13:1-5

Now you understand what Hannah was doing when she said no razor shall touch Samuel's hair. That, in those days, was the life of people set apart unto God. They were known as Nazarites. Samuel was a Nazarite. Now Samson was another Nazarite.

Note carefully here that with Samson, God himself declared the purpose for which he should be set apart unto God, which was to redeem the Israelites from the hands of the Philistines.

See how God empowered Samson and the trouble Samson brought to the Philistines. Some people argue that Samson cut short his purpose by yielding to Delilah's lust; yet, history also shows that Samson's presence while he lived put the Philistines a bit at bay because if they did anything to Israel, God responded through Samson. That was the purpose God gave for Samson's birth.

## John the Baptist

Think also of John the Baptist. He is also one whose birth and purpose was announced by God.

> 12 *And Zechariah was troubled when he saw him, and fear fell upon him.*
>
> 13 *But the angel said to him, "Do not be afraid, Zechariah, for your prayer has been heard, and your wife Elizabeth*

*will bear you a son, and you shall call his name John.*

14 *And you will have joy and gladness, and many will rejoice at his birth,*

15 *for he will be great before the Lord. And he must not drink wine or strong drink, and he will be filled with the Holy Spirit, even from his mother's womb.*

16 *And he will turn many of the children of Israel to the Lord their God,*

17 *and he will go before him in the spirit and power of Elijah, to turn the hearts of the fathers to the children, and the disobedient to the wisdom of the just, to make ready for the Lord a people prepared."*

Luke 1:12-17

John's life looked a bit weird to people because he spent time in the wilderness. Following his life, however, it was clear that he was a child of purpose, and truly he fulfilled that purpose. His ministry stands out today as one who paved the way for the Messiah. That was how God wanted it, and that was how God did it.

## Jesus Christ

Jesus was the greatest Nazarite who lived. Jesus was born for a purpose. He was set apart for something that would benefit the entire world.

Even at the tender age of 12, Jesus knew that He was set apart unto God. The account by Saint Luke makes this clear.

> 46 *After three days they found him in the temple, sitting among the teachers, listening to them and asking them questions.*
>
> 47 *And all who heard him were amazed at his understanding and his answers.*

⁴⁸ And when his parents saw him, they were astonished. And his mother said to him, "Son, why have you treated us so? Behold, your father and I have been searching for you in great distress."

⁴⁹ And he said to them, "Why were you looking for me? Did you not know that I must be in my Father's house?"

⁵⁰ And they did not understand the saying that he spoke to them.

Luke 2:46-50

It is interesting that when Jesus told His parents that He "must be about His Father's business," His parents did not understand Him.

The other instance when Jesus affirmed His being set apart was when He read the scroll in the Synagogue.

16  And he came to Nazareth, where he had been brought up. And as was his custom, he went to the synagogue on the Sabbath day, and he stood up to read.

17  And the scroll of the prophet Isaiah was given to him. He unrolled the scroll and found the place where it was written,

18  "The Spirit of the Lord is upon me, because he has anointed me to proclaim good news to the poor. He has sent me to proclaim liberty to the captives and recovering of sight to the blind, to set at liberty those who are oppressed,

19  to proclaim the year of the Lord's favor."

20  And he rolled up the scroll and gave it back to the attendant and sat

*down. And the eyes of all in the synagogue were fixed on him.*

21 *And he began to say to them, "Today this Scripture has been fulfilled in your hearing*

Luke 4:16-21

This time when He had come of age and recognized by Jewish standards as a man, Jesus expanded what He told His parents when He was only 12 years old. If you watch Jesus closely throughout His earthly ministry, He never lost focus concerning the purpose of His coming into the world.

He stuck to it His whole life: through the Garden of Gethsemane; to the cross; then the resurrection; and then He ascended back to the place from where He had come.

## Paul

We know the story of Paul the apostle, initially Saul of Tarsus. He previously was the chief persecutor of the early church. In his mind, he was doing the work of God because he saw the early church as committing blasphemy by teaching about Jesus being God's way of salvation.

God called him on the way to Damascus on a mission to arrest Christians to bring them up for persecution. He ended up being the greatest missionary of Bible times and a writer of more than half the New Testament. This just means that for all the time he was persecuting the church, he still was someone God had set apart for taking the gospel to many nations.

Have you considered that you could be a Samuel, a Samson, a John the Baptist, or a 21st century Paul?

# It is possible that I could be set apart like...

_____

[Man's Name]

**2.**

# THE LIFE OF A NAZARITE:

# ONE SET APART

If you look again closely at the life of the Nazarites discussed earlier, you get an idea of what it means to be set apart for God. One that stands out clearly is that it is a life of chastity. It means your life is expected to be above all in holiness.

This is clear when you look at the things Nazarites are not supposed to do. That is where the idea of being set apart is established. You cannot do just anything. Being a Nazarite comes with a lot of prohibitions. In other words, things in which you are not to engage.

Take Samson, for example. His strength was located in obedience to not cutting his hair. The moment he disobeyed that instruction he gave his life away. Note well that there is no sin in cutting your hair. It is not the cutting of his hair that brought Samson trouble. It is the disobedience. You know how his story ended.

I know there will be people who believe there is something spiritual about long hair because a lot of God's servants had long hair. I don't think it is about the hair. It was about obedience. It was not the eating of the fruit that got humanity in trouble; after all God created fruits to be eaten by man.

It is Adam's disobedience that brought us the trouble. Notice that Jesus Christ our Lord, also referred to as the Second Adam, cancelled the first Adam's disobedience through obedience, thanks to the prayer in the Garden of Gethsemane.

This simple illustration shows that when you are set apart for God, there are things others may do that may not attract serious punishment, but could land you in God's bad books if you engaged in them. The other side of it is that when you are a Nazarite, some things God may not do with all others, He will do with you. Being set apart unto God has its own principles, demands, and expectations that sometimes may not make sense to the ordinary human mind, but in the end proves to be a wonderful experience.

> **When God gives an instruction, stop thinking about the logic of the instruction. The whole thing is about obedience. Lives set apart for God are characterized by simple obedience.**

## NAZARITES UNDER THE NEW TESTAMENT

If you don't read and interpret the Old Testament carefully you will conclude that only Nazarites are expected to live a life of separation. If the Old Testament represents the shadow of things and the New Testament represents the reality of the shadows, then we need to understand being set apart as under the New Testament.

Paul writing to Timothy gave a gist of the implications of being set apart. Let's turn to that Scripture now and get the message:

> ²⁰ *Now in a great house there are not only vessels of gold and silver but*

also of wood and clay, some for honorable use, some for dishonorable.

21 Therefore, if anyone cleanses himself from what is dishonorable,[d] he will be a vessel for honorable use, set apart as holy, useful to the master of the house, ready for every good work.

22 So flee youthful passions and pursue righteousness, faith, love, and peace, along with those who call on the Lord from a pure heart.

23 Have nothing to do with foolish, ignorant controversies; you know that they breed quarrels.

24 And the Lord's servant must not be quarrelsome but kind to everyone, able to teach, patiently enduring evil,

²⁵ *correcting his opponents with gentleness*

2 Timothy 2:20-25

Let us pause for a bit and make a clarification here. We are living under a different dispensation today. Since the Holy Spirit was poured upon all humanity, we all have become set apart for God. The apostle Paul who wrote to Timothy about vessels teaches that we should come out from amongst the world and be separate.

14 *Do not be unequally yoked with unbelievers. For what partnership has righteousness with lawlessness? Or what fellowship has light with darkness?*

15 *What accord has Christ with Belial? Or what portion does a believer share with an unbeliever?*

16 *What agreement has the temple of God with idols? For we are the*

*temple of the living God; as God said,*
*"I will make my dwelling among*
*them and walk among them, and I*
*will be their God, and they shall be*
*my people.*

<sup>17</sup> *Therefore go out from their midst,*
*and be separate from them, says the*
*Lord, and touch no unclean thing;*
*then I will welcome you,*

<sup>18</sup> *and I will be a father to you, and you*
*shall be sons and daughters to me,*
*says the Lord Almighty.*

2 Corinthians 6:14-18

God is calling us to a life of purity, so we will stand out as different from the world. That is what Nazarites do; they stand out as God's special servants. Under the New Testament, we all have become separated from the world unto God.

Jesus had earlier on said of the disciples that they are in the world, but not of the world. The two are clearly different. We dwell in the world. The world is the physical environment of the earth, but we are not of the world, i.e., the system of beliefs, rules, regulations, and lifestyle that are initiated and influenced by Satan and demons. We are not under satanic influence. We are under the influence of the Holy Spirit.

Note again that the same Apostle Paul speaking to young people wrote this passage to Timothy:

> 22 *So flee youthful passions and pursue righteousness, faith, love, and peace, along with those who call on the Lord from a pure heart.*
> 23 *Have nothing to do with foolish, ignorant controversies; you know that they breed quarrels.*
>
> 2 Timothy 2:22-23

As a young growing person, you have a lot of things going on around you. The question is this:

"What are the things that constitute youthful passions in this 21$^{st}$ century?"

If you pause, use the space below and make your own list, or discuss with your Christian friends what these are today, you will have a whole lot of things that the Bible has not specifically identified by name as evil; for example, addiction to drugs.

1.

2.

3.

4.

5.

6.

7.

8.

9.

10.

The trouble today is that the world is daily introducing so many things that easily pass for youthful passions and it takes the spirit of discernment to identify the dangers in them. The current battle for most youth is whether they should participate in these or not.

> **The sad thing about the church and, for that matter, young growing Christians is that instead of setting examples for the world to follow, we have become engaged in waiting for the world to take the lead in something, and then we struggle as to whether to participate or not.**

We know what technology is doing to the world today, especially the youth and some young adults. Technology is a tool we invented to make doing certain things easier for us.

For example, we do not have to swim when traveling to another part of God's green earth. We drive, sail, or fly in an airplane. We know, however, that the same technology is setting families apart, marketing unwholesome materials to you today in various forms. Youth are becoming so addicted to their phones and other gadgets they are living in a paranoid world created by these gadgets.

Have you thought of the kind of good things that will come your way if you set yourself apart unto God early in life? As you think about this, I want you to drop the idea that as you grow, many things will automatically fall into place for you.

That is a myth. Life does not happen that way. The things that will fall into place for you are the things that you give attention to and commit your time and effort to, drawing from the abundant and readily available grace of God.

Don't wait for some time to come. The time is now. This is the time you decide to come out from amongst the world and be separate unto God as a young person.

It may interest you to know that contrary to some commonly held beliefs, youth are not just hopelessly floating in a world that is bombarding them with all kinds of things. There are young people today who are genuinely seeking to know the truth about God and to follow Him. They are looking for examples to follow. The examples they can most easily identify are young people who love Jesus and are daily walking with Him and testifying to the difference Jesus makes in one's life. Can God count on you to provide that example?

Can you imagine what life will look like for you in the future, if today you have set yourself apart unto God and are providing a good example for the people in your age bracket? It means you have set your foot on a path whose end is never ever in sight. When it ends, you will be safe in the arms of your Creator, Maker, and Savior, who will welcome you with a great smile and give you the ultimate reward He has for you.

# I can provide a good example for my peers by doing the following:

_____

_____

_____

_____

_____

# 3.

# OVERCOMING YOUTHFUL TEMPTATIONS

The greatest pressure to conform to the world is happening in the life of the youth. This is so because they are more vulnerable than the adults. The adults most likely have participated in some of the things the world offers and have seen the bitter results, so they do not want to give those things a second thought again, let alone participating in them.

Youth is often perceived as the age of experimentation. This means young people engage in wanting to try the unknown to see what it looks like. Though it is often said that experience is the best teacher, it is equally dangerous to resign yourself to learn everything by experience.

You wouldn't experiment with what would happen to you if you drank cyanide, for example. By the time you learned the results of that experiment, we would be at your funeral. You would not be alive to write the findings of that experiment.

I once heard someone talk about a process a father wanted to use to teach his young son never to trust anyone. This is what he did. He made his son stand on an elevated position and asked him to jump, saying he would catch him. He jumped and the father did not. You know the result; his son had a mighty fall. Then he told him, "Now you know you cannot trust any man." That was obviously an awful way to let someone learn by experience.

> **Never ever yield to the idea that unless you experience something yourself, it cannot become knowledge for you to live by. Simply take God's word. It is already proven and tested for several generations.**

Sincerely desire to be God's example to your generation. God will help you to make it happen.

## KEEPING YOURSELF PURE

The Psalmist provides the foundation that will help young people live by God's standards. This is what he wrote:

⁹ *How can a young man keep his way pure? By guarding it according to your word.*

¹⁰ *With my whole heart I seek you; let me not wander from your commandments!*

¹¹ *I have stored up your word in my heart, that I might not sin against you.*

¹² *Blessed are you, O LORD; teach me your statutes!*

¹³ *With my lips I declare all the rules of your mouth.*

¹⁴ *In the way of your testimonies I delight as much as in all riches.*

¹⁵ *I will meditate on your precepts and fix my eyes on your ways.*

¹⁶ *I will delight in your statutes; I will not forget your word.*

Psalm 119:9-16

The Psalmist raised an important question and provided the answer. He acknowledged what young people go through and his response was on point for all young, growing people. Every young person should pray this prayer until this Psalm becomes his lifestyle; that God's word will abound in his heart, enable him to become strong in the might of the Lord, and thereby not sin against God.

**Living a life free from sin is the life of someone set apart unto God. When you come out from amongst the world and become separate [set apart] the life you live glorifies God each time.**

The Bible further teaches that all the temptations that come our way are not beyond our ability to overcome them. The Apostle Paul teaches that God does not allow us to be tempted beyond what we can stand, and with every temptation He has provided a way of escape, so we can handle them.

> <sup>12</sup> *Therefore let anyone who thinks that he stands take heed lest he fall.*
>
> <sup>13</sup> *No temptation has overtaken you that is not common to man. God is faithful, and he will not let you be tempted beyond your ability, but with the temptation he will also provide the way of escape, that you may be able to endure it.*
>
> 1 Corinthians 10:12-13

What the passage implies also is that each time we fall to any temptation, we did not see ourselves above the temptation, i.e., equipped to be able to deal with it.

It also means that we do not use the way of escape that God provides. If we start practicing these two, we will be on the way to experience victory over all the temptations that the devil brings our way, whether directly or sometimes through our peers.

The other verse that affirms I Corinthians 10:13 is found in the letter of James to the churches

> 12    *Blessed is the man who remains steadfast under trial, for when he has stood the test he will receive the crown of life, which God has promised to those who love him.*
>
> 13    *Let no one say when he is tempted, "I am being tempted by God," for God cannot be tempted with evil, and he himself tempts no one.*
>
> 14    *But each person is tempted when he is lured and enticed by his own desire.*
>
> 1    *Then desire when it has conceived gives birth to sin, and sin when it is fully grown brings forth death.*
>
> James 1:12-15

James is a bit more detailed in describing how we eventually yield to temptation and sin. Let me illustrate with one example. When you ensure that you are in a room with someone of the opposite sex, most of the time, with doors closed. The initial purpose of your meeting may be good, like learning together to pass an exam, or even praying and having Bible studies. Because you meet very often, just the two of you, a relationship develops naturally between the two of you.

As the relationship develops, your emotions begin to unite in a way different from how you relate with all others of the opposite sex. Once your emotions unite and you are in a place all by yourselves, the stage is set that makes it difficult for you to not touch each other in erotic ways, and that is the beginning of trouble. That is what James means when he says you are drawn from your own lust and enticed.

I am sure you have heard stories of a brother and sister who started having Bible studies all by themselves and even praying together all by themselves and the relationship ended in something else; they had sex in the same place they were having the Bible studies and praying.

Clearly, staying in the same room with someone of the opposite sex all by yourselves is a recipe for eventually having sex, when that was not the initial plan. You are not superhuman; so, it is wise to avoid such situations, thinking you are only doing something as good as praying together.

It is equally not healthy for a young person to constantly look at nude pictures of the opposite sex and think you are just looking at pictures. Your heart and mind become filled with those images instead of God's word and images of Christian character and service. It is not *if*; it is only a matter of *when* you will become addicted to sex and your life will become messed up.

# 4.

# DON'T GET ENTANGLED

¹ *You then, my child, be strengthened by the grace that is in Christ Jesus,*

² *and what you have heard from me in the presence of many witnesses entrust to faithful men, who will be able to teach others also.*

³ *Share in suffering as a good soldier of Christ Jesus.*

⁴ *No soldier gets entangled in civilian pursuits, since his aim is to please the one who enlisted him*

2 Timothy 2:1-4

The passage above is one of Paul's writings to Timothy, who was considered a young Pastor. It is about not getting entangled. To get entangled is to be involved in so many issues that have the potential of taking you off what you are actually expected to channel your energies and resources into. When you get entangled, your focus is shifted to too many issues.

Sometimes those issues are not necessarily evil, but they make it difficult for you to be effective in something very critical to your progress and welfare at a point in time.

We are familiar with the expression, "jack of all trades, but master of none." It presents the picture of someone trying to do everything and, in the process, is unable to do anyone of them very well.

To reinforce the importance of not getting entangled, the Apostle Paul uses the illustration of a soldier. The work of a soldier is primarily to defend his country in times of attack from an enemy who comes against the country with soldiers armed with ammunition.

The common experience we have with soldiers is that they usually live in barracks. The barracks are specialized environments created for them. They are removed from civilian populations. The idea is that they want soldiers to focus on their mission. They could be called at any time to defend their country when the need arises, and that will not be the time they have other things on their minds.

Paul says that they are shielded from being entangled with civilian issues, and the idea is to please their Commander in Chief, i.e., the President or the leader of their country. Serving your country in that regard is considered one of the highest callings for a citizen. Soldiers' lives are forever tied to the security of their country, even to the point of losing their lives.

Can you imagine that at the time you are writing exams your friends want you to go out to watch movies, or go to the beach, or visit some place of keen interest to you?

Those activities may not necessarily be evil, but if at the time you are writing exams you get involved in them, they become entanglements and they rob you of having a good revision and preparation to enable you to pass your exams well. At the time that you should be in your books you are watching your favorite movie and having all the emotional fun in the theater. You never feel sad watching your most favorable movie, but in the process, you are sacrificing good grades for poor performance. That can't take you to the next phase of your academic and career path.

**The ability to discern which activities are generally not evil but become entanglements in the face of major pursuits in your life is a sign of great maturity.**

Paul considers the Christian life a higher call, and the Person we desire to please in this call is God, who saved and cleansed and delivered us from sin and all its results. He is the same God who is seeking partnership with us to accomplish something great for the kingdom of God on earth.

## LOVE NOT THE WORLD

The entanglement mentality calls for a separation from what is happening around so you can focus on the principal thing for your life. Here, I will deal with it in general terms. The Apostle John wrote to the church and gave this warning about getting involved with the world:

> 15 *Do not love the world or the things in the world. If anyone loves the world, the love of the Father is not in him.*
>
> 16 *For all that is in the world—the desires of the flesh and the desires of the eyes and pride of life—is not from the Father but is from the world.*

17    And the world is passing away along with its desires, but whoever does the will of God abides forever.

1 John 2:15-17

18    If the world hates you, know that it has hated me before it hated you.

19    If you were of the world, the world would love you as its own; but because you are not of the world, but I chose you out of the world, therefore the world hates you.

20    Remember the word that I said to you: 'A servant is not greater than his master.' If they persecuted me, they will also persecute you. If they kept my word, they will also keep yours.

21    But all these things they will do to you on account of my name, because they do not know him who sent me.

John 15:18-21

Here's also what the apostle James wrote about the same issue.

> *You adulterous people! Do you not know that friendship with the world is enmity with God? Therefore, whoever wishes to be a friend of the world makes himself an enemy of God.*

> James 4:4

These constitute two powerful witnesses. Let their testimony establish the truth about separating yourself from the world and let the experience of setting yourself apart from the world become a real and meaningful experience for you at this stage of your life.

What the Bible describes as the world is a system of thoughts, patterns, attitudes and behaviors that are contrary to God's word and His principles. The world, in this sense, is not the geographical location where humanity lives now.

It is a system that has Satan at the helm of affairs. He influences and sometimes dictates to the people he has held in captive what he wants to happen on God's earth.

1. Take for example, fashion. People are expected to dress decently. Today, we have people who will endorse for a woman to wear a dress that shows her breasts openly and they describe her as sexy. This is a typical dressing that is described as worldly because it goes against Christian principles of decency.

   The world wants you to show to everyone what, in God's principle, must be reserved for the one you will spend your life together in holy matrimony. Today, in many university campuses around the country the issue of dress code is an issue because there are those who think ladies are adults and should be allowed to wear anything that feels good.

2. Some people who work as accountants, for example, use their knowledge to falsify information to their advantage. Some think they are being smart, but in the Christian principles of accounting, this is evil in the sight of God.

3. In an academic setting for example students are presented with all kinds of offers, including lecturers requesting sex from students so they will reward them with grades they have not worked for.

    Those who go for that offer appear smart because they are given high grades, and everyone sees them as brilliant students. In fact, their behavior is considered the norm for the times we are in.

4. Those who do not take the offer from corrupt lecturers are often called different names. They are considered stupid or that they are

not using their God-given senses for their good. The truth is that by not participating in those games, they demonstrated that they are different. They showed their commitment to God.

5. A lot of young people are introduced to friendships with the same sex, commonly called boys-boys and, if you like, girls-girls. Very often the conversations that go on in these settings when they come together is not edifying enough.

Young people are made to think that this is the "in-thing" now. For fear they will be branded outmoded if they abstain, they get involved anyhow. Then, they discover that they are gradually giving up the virtues of life that affirm their position as set apart for God in their generation. They disobey what they have learned from Godly parents and from church principles.

# 5.

# THE BLESSINGS OF A LIFE OF PURITY

¹  Blessed is the man who walks not
in the counsel of the wicked, nor
stands in the way of sinners, nor sits
in the seat of scoffers;

²  but his delight is in the law of
the LORD, and on his law he
meditates day and night.

³  He is like a tree planted by streams of
water that yields its fruit in its
season, and its leaf does not wither.
In all that he does, he prospers

Psalm 1:1-3

What every young person should know is that
a life of purity is precious in the sight of God. He
honors holiness and purity anywhere He finds it.

This first psalm is for many seasons and for
many situations in this life. It comes quite handy
when we talk of the blessings of a pure life. It is
clearly a psalm for a life of separation and being set

apart unto God. The first part identifies what it means to separate oneself from ungodly people and situations. It ends by identifying the position destined for the man who sets himself apart. His delight is in the law of the Lord and on His law, he spends time morning, noon, and night.

The second part of the passage identifies what good comes to the person who sets himself apart by not participating in the evil ways of men. He grows, always fresh because he draws his strength for daily living from staying in God's presence and being deeply engrossed with God's word. He prospers in all he does.

He is always fresh with ideas for succeeding in what he sets himself to do because of God's continual presence with him.

Too many young people today lack knowledge of the word of God. They have all kinds of things stored in their minds and hearts, but little space for the word of God. It is time to go back and live according to the exhortation of the Psalmist.

Listen to what Jesus Himself said about purity in heart:

> *"Blessed are the pure in heart, for they shall see God!"*
>
> Matthew 5:8

To be pure is to overcome all conscious sins that you are tempted with so that you can stand before God's face with a clear conscience.

Keeping yourself pure involves keeping your thoughts and heart to that which you know from God's word to be good and right. It involves checking your actions and making sure they are of the right motive.

Purity also helps you constantly evaluate what thoughts and feelings run through your soul as you go through each day. It places you in position to choose to think only about the things that will please God and make you happy.

**When you walk in any of the manifestations of impurity, it affects your relationship with God. You lack the confidence to go to God even though God has always said His arms are open to receive all who come to Him.**

Purity guarantees that you are not easily drawn into waywardness.

Keeping yourself pure is a choice that you make, it is not a gift you receive from God; so, everyone can be pure in heart. God will not stand in your way if you choose to keep yourself pure. The benefits of purity are numerous and for as long as you walk in purity, there is no way you are going to miss any of them. Find below a few of them:

## A GOOD CONSCIENCE!

If you are able to keep your mind and heart pure, you experience a clear conscience all the time. The experience of a clear conscience is that you are free from guilt and worry about the decisions you are making and the direction you are taking your life. Your conscience is God's voice to you directly.

Your conscience constantly tells you what is right and what is wrong. When you are pure, your conscience does little of warning you of something wrong you are going to do. Very often your conscience will do a lot more of affirmation because out of purity you are doing most of what God expects.

You are thinking God's thoughts, developing Godly attitudes, and performing God's acts. You experience good judgement in the issues that confront you.

## FACING LIFE MORE CONFIDENTLY

When your mind and heart are pure, it becomes difficult for your perceptions of life to be darkened. You walk in perpetual enlightenment. For this reason, you are able to walk through life with greater certainty. You become more confident that God is with you every step of the way both in your decisions and in the pursuit of your dreams. The Bible has said that the righteous are as bold as the lion. When you walk in purity you become as bold as the lion. Nothing threatens you because you know that God is with you all the time.

When Paul wrote about the fruit of the Spirit in Galatians 5:22-24, he added that "against these there is no law." What that means is that when you walk in them, you do not look over your shoulders to see if someone is watching you. You know you are in the right way and you walk chest out.

## YOU BECOME ALMOST INCORRUPTIBLE

Because of the purity of your heart, whatever you hear is filtered by a purified conscience. One of the great blessings associated with this is that it becomes difficult for you to be drawn into bad morals. Your thoughts, feelings, and behaviors are shielded from most of the negative influences around you. You end up being freed from many of the unacceptable behaviors that today's youth are struggling to free themselves from.

In the process, you save yourself from many of the difficulties your peers go through. They cannot tell you to sell your body for grades if you are a female student, for example.

## NO MORE DOUBLE MINDEDNESS

When your thoughts are always pure, you experience what is called single-mindedness. It means for most of the time, you don't toggle between two or more opinions over a single issue of life. You focus on one side of morality and then struggle with what is right or wrong.

What I am trying to get you to understand here is that a pure mind is free from unhealthy alternate thoughts. Too many alternate thoughts often land people into all kinds of trouble. They also get you frozen and unable to make decisions to move forward with your life.

## ASSURANCE OF HEAVEN

Even though we do not earn heaven by our good works but by the death and resurrection of Jesus Christ our Lord, it is not uncommon to find Christians who sometimes doubt if they are going to heaven when they leave this world.

Most of it has to do with the kind of life they are living even though they are children of God. This will not be the case with those who keep a pure heart. You are able to lay hold on the gift of eternal life that is yours in Christ.

The Bible has said that all those who love the appearing of our Lord Jesus Christ to take us home keep themselves pure, as Jesus is pure. It means that purity makes a person always assured of living with Jesus one day.

# 6.

# YOUR PERSONAL NAZARITE VOW

> ¹ *Therefore, since we are surrounded by so great a cloud of witnesses, let us also lay aside every weight, and sin which clings so closely, and let us run with endurance the race that is set before us,*
>
> ² *looking to Jesus, the founder and perfecter of our faith, who for the joy that was set before him endured the cross, despising the shame, and is seated at the right hand of the throne of God.*

Hebrews 12:1-2

If you critically study the passage above from the book of Hebrews, you can see two exhortations to anyone who is a Nazarite.

The first is separating yourself from what are obvious as sins. These are attitudes and behaviors that the Bible has categorically identified as wrong in the sight of God. Many of us are familiar with sins because that is what we have been warned about from the day we learned to speak. Your parents have told you what is right and what is wrong. You have heard it from your youth pastor and your senior pastor. As you read this section, I am sure some of them are running through your mind.

The second item identified represents those things that do not look like sins but are entanglements. You know what entanglements do to a soldier, and a Christian for that matter. That is what the Bible calls weights.

An athlete can run a race wearing a suit and shoes and having some coins in his pocket. He can also decide to run the race wearing a simple singlet, shorts, and a canvas designed for running. You know the difference it makes. One is running light, the other is running with weights. No one will penalize him running the race with weights, but you know the results. You cannot run and win with weights.

We are usually not very familiar with weights and, so very often, we unknowingly carry weights of different kinds.

The power of weights is that they often do not look like sins. The other way to describe weights is the appearance of evil. Some weights are actually what the Bible calls the appearance of evil.

If we allow our lives to be dominated by appearance of evil, we cease to become the people set apart unto God. We are unable to represent God the best way we can.

## MAKING IT VERY PERSONAL

With the understanding of the life of a Nazarite, and the fact that under the New Testament we who are saved by Christ have all become Nazarites, I want you to do a very simple exercise: You can write down your personal Nazarite vow. Write it in the form of a declaration. Write it such that each time you look at it, you will be driven to run for only that which matters, avoiding those things that tend to keep you in bondage again. Follow this guide:

1. List the common sins that youth commit and pledge with God that none of them should be found lurking in your life; that as soon as any of them shows up they will be eliminated. These are thoughts, attitudes and behaviors that clearly do not describe you as a Nazarite, set apart unto God.

**1.**

**2.**

**3.**

**4.**

**5.**

**6.**

**7.**

2. Write the things that look good to everyone but have the appearance of evil. Things that others may find okay but by your conscience you know that these are things God wants you to do as His special child.

1.

2.

3.

4.

5.

6.

7.

As you make the list of what you should abstain from, don't wait for anyone to tell you what to take out of your life. If you do a good and comprehensive list under the guidance of the Holy Spirit, you will realize that you are more than Samuel, Samson, John the Baptist, or any other

Bible character whose birth was announced and who was declared a Nazarite.

Whatever things go on that list, do remember to take them one-by-one to prayer constantly and trust the Holy Spirit to work with you until, by the grace of God, you get the unacceptable ones completely out of your life.

At the same time pray that the thoughts, attitudes and behaviors that describe you as one set apart unto God will be formed in your life. Give yourself time because growing into the image of Christ does not happen overnight.

What you have to understand is that nothing about human development happens in a rush. It is not because God does not want to help you quickly. It is just that life is a process and processes have their own time frames that are often difficult to alter. God takes you through situations in life to purify you and make you look really good in His sight.

Most young people living in this microwave generation want to skip the process. You cannot skip the process and expect to get God's best. Waiting on God is a good way to eliminate all that went into your Nazarite vow.

I trust that you have understood this principle of setting yourself apart unto God and you are ready to commit your heart and mind to living exclusively for Jesus, who loves you and gave His life to save you. That is the one sure way you can show your gratitude to Him, and it is great to do that while you are still going through the youthful years of your life, before the evil days come.

I declare to you that the power of God will overshadow you and open your eyes to see the riches God has in store for those who love Him and yield to His will and purpose.

I pray that you will hear many things around you but you will listen only to the Holy Spirit. You will see your peers doing so many things to just fit in, but your story will be different. For you, it shall be said that you are a different breed; and it will all be according to the God of heaven, who has favored you and brought you into partnership with Himself to use you to reach out to several in your generation.

God bless you!

# "Here I Am, Lord. I am available, and at Your service, Lord."

_____

[Name]

_____

[Date]

www.ingramcontent.com/pod-product-compliance
Lightning Source LLC
Chambersburg PA
CBHW071818020426
42331CB00007B/1526